Ioana Chicet-Macoveiciuc
The Naked Truth. Funny dialogues about one's body and privacy, strangers and limits

© Editura Univers, 2018
All Rights Reserved

Collection: UNICORN UNIVERS
Coordinator: Ioana Chicet-Macoveiciuc
Editor: Diana Crupenschi
Layout: Constantin Niță
Proofreading: Irinel Antoniu

IOANA CHICET-MACOVEICIUC

The Naked Truth

Funny dialogues about one's body privacy, strangers and limits

Illustrations by
IONUȚ ROBERT OLARU

Translated from Romanian by PETRU IAMANDI

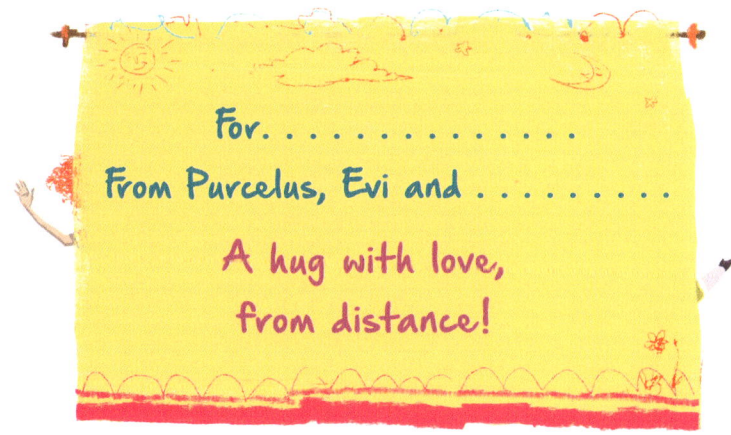

EDITURA UNIVERS

Evi and the Smartest Little Pig

When Evi turned three, he was given Purcelus as a birthday gift. He liked him at once. It was obvious Purcelus was not an ordinary stuffed animal. Well, he was quite small and very fluffy, like all stuffed animals. But he had very clever eyes and sometimes seemed to be moving his ears and little tail, curled like a ring. He was dressed in a T-shirt with a pod in the middle, and pants like a capsicum. He was crazy about food, snored loudly – oink, oink – and was very smart.

Now would you like to know something about Evi too? Well, Evi was a very curious kid. Like you. He kept asking a lot of questions about everything as he wanted to understand everything as quickly as possible. Evi's parents did not always manage to find answers to his questions so, when he turned three, they went into a shop and asked:

"What is the smartest toy you've got?"

"We've got several books which are very smart and a block game, but the cleverest is this little pig dressed in capsicum-like pants. He knows everything about anything!" answered a pretty red-haired saleswoman.

So Evi's parents bought it immediately.

Mummy tied a red ribbon to his small tail and Evi was so happy when he got him on the morning of his birthday.

Then there was a birthday party that all Evi's friends attended; they played games, ate pizza and a big cake, frolicked and competed against each other – who could draw the most beautiful horse, so Evi couldn't spend too much time with the smart little pig.

But at night, when the party was over and there was not a crumb of cake left, Evi went to bed after brushing his teeth, of course. He put the little pig on a pillow next to his and, after Mummy switched off the light, he said:

"I know you're a stuffed animal but I'll talk to you anyway because I'm a child and that's what children do, they talk to their toys."

To his amazement, Purcelus whispered to him:

"Oink, meaning hi, buddy! I'm so glad you're talking to me! It's hard to be a talking little stuffed pig. Children get scared most of the times and their parents are afraid I know more than they do."

"Do you know many things?" asked Evi, lying more comfortably under the blanket.

"I know lots of things," answered the little stuffed pig, proudly. "I know, for instance, who the smartest animals in the world are!"

"Pigs?" asked Evi quickly.

"Oh, no, chimps! But pigs are smart too!" answered Purcelus, smacking his lips.

"I didn't know pigs are that smart. I fact, I thought little of pigs, Mummy says they're dirty," said Evi a little ashamed.

"Well, it's true we're a little bit untidy but that's only because our minds are busy with something else," explained the little pig.

"I like you a lot," said Evi smiling. "And I'm so glad you're my new friend. What's your name?"

'My name is Purcelus. With an *s* not *sh*. And with the stress on *ce* not on *lus*. Repeat after me: Pur-CE-lus."

"PurCElus, with an *s*, I've got it. And I am Evi. You can call me whatever you want, I will still be Evi."

"Good night, Evi, glad to meet you."

"Sleep well, Purcelus! Tomorrow I'm going to ask you a lot of questions," said Evi before he fell asleep.

"And I'm going to ask for food," the little pig warned him. "I love eating. And please take me with you wherever you go because I've got so

many things to tell you about the world. And because I'm afraid of being alone. But don't say that to anyone," whispered the little pig and fell asleep at once, snoring loudly: oink, oink, oink ...

It so happened that Evi and Purcelus became inseparable. Evi would take the wise little pig everywhere, holding him by one of his legs, ears or tail. He would put Purcelus next to him in the car, with the seatbelt on, at the table or at the

theatre. They would talk all the time, point to whatever they saw around them, laugh and sometimes even disagree on this and that until late into the night, under the blanket.

They would go together through lots of adventures and somebody has written this book so you can discover them too.

Come with Me to the Bathroom!

One Saturday morning, while his parents were still asleep, Evi went to the bathroom and took Purcelus along, but Purcelus refused to go in.

"Hey, what are you up to, piggy, leaving me all by myself in the bathroom?"

"You know, Evi, when it comes to bathrooms, it's every man for himself".

"But I get bored to stay there alone. That's why I never leave Mummy alone in the bathroom. Whenever she goes in, I'm there too, to keep her company."

Purcelus was staring at him, with his front legs crossed on his chest.

"Evi, I'm sure your Mummy would rather be alone in the bathroom."

"Really? I've never thought of that. Why would one like to be alone in the bathroom?" asked Evi looking very thoughtful from beneath his messy hair.

"First because in the bathroom more often than not you pull down your pants to poop or pee. And your butt and private parts are only for you to see. That's the rule."

"But apart from me, it's only Mummy that sees them," said Evi scratching an ear.

"Oink! Well, while you still need to be washed and dressed, Mummy can see you naked. But a few years from now, when you are older and can do it by yourself, only you should see your private parts," explained the little pig seriously.

"But I don't mind being seen without clothes."

"I know, I don't mind it either. But that's the rule and it's important to obey it. Look, I wear pants even though I'm a pig. If I have to live among people, then I must obey their rules. They don't show their private parts to each other. When I go back to the pigs' world, I'll be allowed to stay naked, because that's the custom. With people, you must wear clothes."

"I get it. But can I keep the door open while I'm brushing my teeth? That takes quite a while and I'm so bored with nobody around," said Evi sulkily.

"Why not, while you're brushing your teeth or washing your face you can leave the door open and I can show you how a gracious little pig can dance like a ballerina."

"OK, but now I hope you don't mind if I shut the door – I want to pee."

And the little stuffed pig waited patiently outside until Evi finished his personal business in the bathroom.

Then they went to the kitchen to fill their bowls with milk and cereals. The little pig snouted everything from his bowl while Evi used, daintily, the milk spoon. When they finished eating, Evi and Purcelus played Monopoly. The little pig won but Evi didn't mind.

The Secret

Later the same day the whole family was excited: they were about to go on their seaside vacation. When he learned that, Purcelus hid under the wardrobe oinking desperately. After Evi pulled him out, the little pig said he was ill, hoping they would leave him at home.

"What's the matter, why are you so nervous, don't you want to go with us to the seaside?" asked Evi, worriedly.

"Oink! I don't want us to go anywhere," answered the little pig hoarsely.

"I'm sorry but we've got to, Mummy and Daddy have already paid for the flight and the hotel. And you can join us for free if you sleep in the same bed with me and promise not to ask for too much food. I wouldn't like to go there without you … you're my best friend!" said Evi holding the little pig so tight the latter's eyes almost popped out.

"Can I tell you a secret?" asked Purcelus in the smallest of voices.

"Of course."

"I'm afraid of flying," confessed Purcelus pushing his snout into Evi's shoulder.

"Oh, I see. I used to be afraid of flying too, before my first flight. But now I love it. Want to know how I got used to it?"

"Did you drink a special syrup that cures the fright?"

"Come on, little pig, there's no such thing. Mummy held me by the hand and told me everything about it, step by step. I trusted her and everything was OK. We'll do the same. I'll hold you in my arms or just take hold of your little tail and we'll have the time of our lives!" promised Evi.

"Deal, but don't tell anybody I'm afraid of flying," said the little pig, joining his front legs as if in a prayer.

"I assure you, little pig, I won't tell anybody. Except Mummy and Daddy. They must know everything I know."

"Oink, couldn't you keep just this little secret for yourself?"

"No, little pig, I'm sorry. Children must share everything with their parents. It's a very important rule,

just like the one about going to the bathroom by yourself, the one *you* mentioned. This is about safety too. I'm too young and something that I don't want to share with Mummy and Daddy may harm me."

"You're right, Evi, you're very smart. Mummy and Daddy must know everything about us. So let's tell them I'm afraid of flying."

"Let's! Mummy's very good at this, you know, she can help you a lot. And it's much better without secrets, you feel so … light!"

The little pig took Evi by the hand and they went to see Mummy who was choosing the right books for the vacation. They told her Purcelus' secret and she assured the little pig everything would be fine; then they felt like eating something. She cooked some sweetcorn and Evi ate it daintily, kernel by kernel, while Purcelus gulped it, as greedy as a pig.

On the Beach

The flight was OK, Purcelus slept like a log on Evi's knees, snoring slowly oink, oink, oink, oink, and so on. Next morning, when he woke up, they were all on the beach. Sometimes that's what pigs are like, they sleep a lot and not even a bomb exploding next to them can wake them up! Just as he opened his eyes he saw Evi perched on a beach chair, wrapped in a towel. Since it wasn't cold at all, the little pig whispered worriedly:

"Evi, why are you sitting there wrapped like a small cabbage roll? Are you ill?"

"No, you snoring little pig. I'm just thinking."

"Forget it, let's paddle in that clear water, with those little fish, wow, pigs love having baths … Oink!"

"Wait, don't go in there without me. We need to talk first," said Evi.

"Dear me, is that why we've come to the seaside? Not to paddle? We could do a lot of talking at home, couldn't we?" said the little pig taking off his capsicum-like pants.

"Little pig, yesterday you told me no-one but Mummy, who washes me, must see me naked, right?" asked Evi seriously.

"Oink, meaning yes," said the little pig looking at the sea.

"I've given it some thought and I believe you're right. But what about lying on the beach? Last year and the years before that I lay here naked, Mummy said I was young enough for that."

"This year, if you want, you can wear your trunks. And in all the years to come," said the little pig quickly.

"What about the swimming pool? Or the locker room at the kindergarten?"

"Everywhere. It's your body, after all. It's up to you. As a rule, when there's company present, be they children or grown-ups, acquaintances or strangers, the rule says we must be wearing something."

"I like that, I'm going to tell Mummy about it. Just wait here …"

But it was too late. The little pig had already dived into the azure waves, chasing the fish, which didn't know what that pink being was, oinking and throwing up bubbles through the snout.

When Evi told Mummy he'd like to wear trunks on the beach, she smiled. She had already bought him a nice pair, as green as the seaweed. Now Evi was feeling much better on the beach, dressed as a grown-up.

Later, Curiously

Towards evening Mummy and Daddy were having a snack while Evi and Purcelus were playing in the sand close by.

"Listen, little pig …"

"You can't find a better listener than me, thank you," replied the little pig using a toothpick to remove a trace of shrimp from his teeth.

Undoubtedly, he was a well-behaved little pig.

"If all of us wear clothes all the time, how can I see what other people look like when they are naked?" asked Evi.

"As a matter of fact, all people look alike, as pigs do. All of them have legs, backs, round butts, curled tails."

"Hey, people don't have tails, little pig!" said Evi laughing.

"Oink. Meaning yes, of course they don't."

"On the other hand, boys look different from girls, Mummy looks different from Daddy," said Evi looking at the sky.

"Well, young hogs look different from young sows, but not much. If you want to know more about it, just ask your Mummy about these differences. You can read together a biology book where you can see drawings of human bodies. Curiosity is natural. But it's not natural to walk naked in the street and for people to see your private parts. Remember the rule?" asked Purcelus.

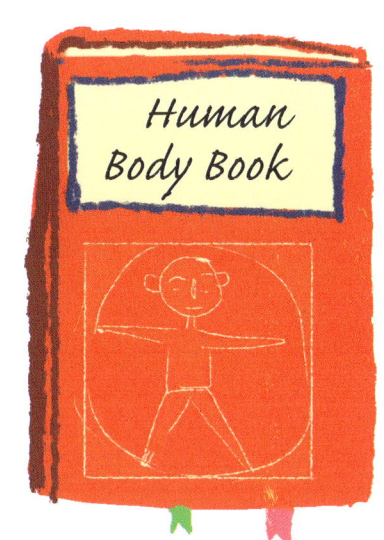

"Yes, I'm the only one to see myself without clothes. But you know something?" asked Evi grubbing the sand.

"I know a lot of things because I'm smart," boasted the little pig.

"Do you fancy an ice-cream?" asked Evi cheerfully.

"It's rather late for that, we'd better get some sleep, tomorrow we'll be on the beach early in the morning!"

The little pig had barely said that when he fell asleep, with his snout in the sand.

In the Park, a Strange Proposal

The seaside vacation over, Evi, his family and pink friend came back home. One day in the park, Mummy was reading a book on a bench while Evi, close to her, was building a castle from leaves and twigs. At first Purcelus played with him but then he started to grub in the sand for acorns.

"Hey, little pig, take it easy or we'll have to put you in the washing machine," said Evi when he noticed the little pig's snout had turned greenish-black.

"Dear me, oh, no, thank you, the last time you took me out of it I was so crumpled, ruffled and dizzy. Oink!" said the little pig holding his head and staggering, about to fall over the pile of twigs.

A few minutes later Evi made friends with a little boy who had a large collection of toy shovels and buckets.

"Mummy, can I go and play with this little boy in the sandbox?"

Mummy agreed, so the two new friends went to the sandbox and started to play. The little pig followed them through the grass, sniffing at a worm. Suddenly, a woman in a red coat stopped in front of them. She had a bag of biscuits in her hand.

"What are you doing here, kids? How would you like a biscuit?"

Evi's Mummy was absorbed by the book and didn't hear the woman

talking to the boys. The one with the shovels and buckets stretched his arm quickly, but Evi couldn't make up his mind. He looked at Purcelus. The little pig, his head patched by dust and leaves, warned him:

"If I were you I wouldn't take anything from a stranger. What if she didn't wash her hands?"

Evi laughed.

"Look who's talking! You're too dirty to teach lessons about cleanliness!"

"Wait, Evi, I'm not kidding. What if the biscuits are stale? Or she dropped

them on the ground on the way here? And how do we know why this woman is offering us something to eat?"

"Well, maybe she's just kind-hearted."

"Oink! Meaning she may be kind-hearted, but the truth is we don't really know anything about those biscuits and why this woman with a funny hat is offering them to us. The safest way is to say *No, thank you,* and then go and tell your Mummy about it. Normally, grown-ups shouldn't try to talk to children unless their Mummy or Daddy is with them," said the little pig shaking his head to get rid of the dirt.

"Is that another important rule?"

"Yes, oink, it is!"

"OK then. But let me tell you it's not good manners to talk to somebody with bits of leaves between your teeth either. Come here, let me brush you a little, I don't want Mummy to see you like that."

Evi and the little pig went back to Mummy who helped them wash their hands and faces and opened her bag to give them each an apple. Evi munched it slowly, while the little pig grabbed and swallowed it and then hiccupped the rest of the day. Hic!

Mummy, Where Are You?

One afternoon Evi got a terrible fright. He was lucky to have Purcelus in his backpack, though. This is what happened:

Evi and Mummy went to a large department store. She was carrying a couple of bags full of vegetables, eggs and milk, so she couldn't hold Evi, who was walking carefully next to her, by the hand. Suddenly Evi stopped to look at a toy train in a window and Mummy walked on, and when the boy looked around, he couldn't see her. He ran left, right and center, shouting:

"Mummy, where are you?"

A lot of grown-ups were passing by. Evi got scared and started to cry. Purcelus, who was sleeping in his backpack and dreaming of fresh carrots, woke up to his cries and started to talk to him, almost in a whisper so the people around couldn't hear him. They would have gotten frightened hearing a little pig talk.

"Evi, hey, Evi, I'm here, with you!"

Evi started, taken aback by the talking backpack but he soon realized the little stuffed pig was there, trying to help him. So he took him out and told him in a rush how he got lost and scared because he didn't know what to do … He was both scared and missed his mother.

"Evi, where was Mummy when you last saw her?"

"Here, next to this window with the toy train in it."

"Right, then let's wait here. If you run to and fro and she's looking for you, she won't be able to find you. If you stay put where she last saw you, she'll come back to you."

"And what if she doesn't come?" asked Evi and started to cry again.

"If she doesn't, we'll look for a person in uniform."

"You mean a firefighter?"

"Oink. Meaning no. A guard or a police officer or an employee. They can use these big loudspeakers to let

everybody know that there's a little boy outside the window with the toy train waiting for his mother. And Mummy will hear it and come here."

"And what if we don't find a person in uniform?" asked Evi.

"Then we ask a Mummy who's here with her child to help us find your Mummy."

"OK, or help us call Mummy."

"Oink. But for that you need to know her phone number."

"I haven't been able to learn it by heart but I've got it written on a piece of paper here, in my backpack. Mummy told me to keep it, in case I get lost …"

"Your Mummy is very smart. Like me," said the little pig smacking his lips with great satisfaction.

While Purcelus was thinking he could do with a little bit of beet, Mummy came running worried and red in the face. As red as a beet, the little pig said to himself.

"Evi, I've been worried sick. Are you all right?"

"Yes, Mummy, relax, Purcelus told me what to do if I get lost. And he suggested next time we go shopping you buy him some beet, he says it makes him snore less loudly."

Mummy hugged Evi, then they left the department store and went to the parking lot. But they forgot to take the little pig who was still standing next to the window with the toy train dreaming of the beet cooked with all sorts of herbs and Parmesan cheese. When he realized he'd been left behind he got scared but soon he understood the best solution was not to panic but wait patiently.

And he was right.

In less than a minute Evi came back running with his arms outstretched.

"I'm sorry, little pig, I got excited and forgot all about you. Let's go home, Mummy's going to make us pasta and leek!"

"Oink! Meaning yum-yum!"

An Anniversary Kiss

Today is Evi's Mummy's birthday. Early in the morning, while she was still in bed, Daddy gave her flowers and a beautiful present, with a big bow on it! Evi also gave his mother a present: a marker-drawn drawing.

There was a heart-shaped house in it and in the house there was the whole family: Mummy, Daddy, Evi and Purcelus, all holding hands and smiling.

Mummy was so excited, especially when Daddy, Evi and the little pig sang "Happy birthday to you!", each in their own way, and Mummy blew out the candle stuck into the cake-shaped omelet Daddy had made.

Then Mummy and Daddy kissed each other. On the lips!

Evi leant over to kiss his mother on the lips too but Purcelus pulled at his pajamas so hard Evi fell on her. They all burst out laughing.

"Purcelus is right, you know," said Mummy. "Only spouses kiss each other on the lips. The prince and the princess, Mummy and Daddy."

"Does that mean you and Daddy are allowed to do it, and you and I are not?" asked Evi with disappointment in his voice.

"Something like that. Your little mouth is only yours, it's not supposed to touch somebody else's."

"But why? Don't we eat ice-cream from the same bucket?" asked Evi scratching his messy hair and feeling like eating some ice-cream.

"You're right, but it's not the same thing. Kissing is one way of showing our love. Daddy and I love in one way, I love you in another, your love for your little pig is different from your love for me. The same goes for kisses. Children must not kiss each other on the mouth. You mustn't do it with your Mummy, Granny or your kindergarten mates. When you've grown up and fallen in love with somebody and want to be with that person, then you can kiss them on the mouth, like Daddy and I do. Is that clear my little ratoon with a sub nose?"

"Crystal clear."

Evi got a big kiss from Mummy on his forehead. Purcelus leant his snout over to Evi's mother for the same thing but she didn't kiss him, just lifted and shook him to help him get rid of some fluffs.

After breakfast, Mummy took them all out for an ice-cream. Purcelus would have liked a cabbage ice-cream but, as they didn't sell anything like that, he was content to have a pistachio one, given it was also green.

A Bath after the Rain

One day Evi woke up from his afternoon nap, looked out of the window and was surprised to see that it had rained a lot, the trees were damp and the street was full of puddles. He ran shouting to the kitchen where Mummy was just taking out a sweet smelling apple pie from the oven:

"Mummy, it's been raining! Now we can go out and splash each other and jump over the puddles! Mummy, it's been raining, it's so cool!"

Mummy glanced at him with a smile then she went to the bedroom to change her clothes. A few minutes later they were out. Evi was spinning like a top in the middle of the largest puddle on the sidewalk. She smiled again seeing how funny Evi looked, playing there, with Purcelus in his arms, the little pig not exactly enjoying the idea of getting wet in a puddle.

"Come on, Mummy, join us. And you, Purcelus, cheer up. It's so cool to get wet!"

"No, thanks," said the little pig politely. "I'd rather be clean and dry when I taste that pie."

He had hardly finished the sentence when Evi grabbed him by his front legs and started to jump on the sidewalk, laughing and making up stories about pirates and medusas. Soon the little pig kicked back and even enjoyed their adventure in the rain. Suddenly he saw a nut which had just dropped into a puddle from a walnut-tree. Without giving it a second thought he jumped on it. A second later the little pig was wet and muddy all over. A broken leaf was hanging from one of his ears.

Evi laughed.

"Hey, Purcelus, just look at the mess you're in!"

"And I haven't even gotten the nut, it just rolled under that car," said the little pig almost crying.

"Let's go home and wash you," said Mummy lifting him from the puddle by his small tail.

They climbed up the steps in a hurry and, once in the bathroom, Evi tried to wash the little pig. But Purcelus stepped back from the shower and said:

"I always wash myself, mind you. I don't want to be seen naked and touched by other people."

Evi stared at him in amazement.

"Mummy always washes me, you know. My butt, everything …"

"I know that, you're just a child. When you get older, you'll do it yourself. You'll surely want to protect your privacy."

"Do you think I'll be able to?"

"Oink! Of course, I mean look at me, though I'm a little pig I can manage it all right."

Evi thought hard. He's right, this little pig, he's so smart!

"Evi, it's only your Mummy or Daddy that can touch you when you're naked. And the doctor, when you've fallen ill and they need to know the cause. And even then your Mummy must be with you. And now please leave me alone, I want to wash myself," added the little pig showing Evi the door with his pink fat leg.

"OK, I've got it," said Evi leaving.

"Oh, one more thing, make sure you have two helpings of apple pie ready for me."

"Two?"

"Oink! A clean pig's appetite is twice bigger than usual. Didn't you know that?"

An Exchange of Clothes

Today Evi is going on a trip with his kindergarten mates. He's putting his things into the backpack excitedly: clothes, a bottle of water and a banana.

"You should take a bowl of soup too, in case you get hungry," says the little pig who always makes sure there's food at hand.

"We're going to visit a castle, Purcelus!"

"Wow, how interesting, I've always wanted to see a castle."

"Unfortunately, I'm not allowed to take any toys with me, that's the rule, you know …"

"Wait a second. Don't tell me I'm a toy. I am a little pig! And your best friend," says Purcelus with tears in his eyes. "I'm going to miss you! Oink!"

"Me too. Listen, how about you lending me something that belongs to you, to remind me of you?"

The little pig looks around, puzzled. He doesn't have too many things that belong to him. He's got only the T-shirt and the pants.

"If I lend you my clothes, I'm going to be cold … Pigs don't like being cold."

"Well, me and my kindergarten mates always exchange clothes," explains Evi.

"Shucks, I for one wouldn't like to wear somebody else's clothes. My skin is very sensitive, you know," says the little pig pulling a funny snout.

"We do like it. It's one way of not getting bored with ours," says Evi waving his arms.

"I hope you don't exchange your undergarments too."

"What's that, little pig?"

"Underwear. It covers the private parts."

"Oh, no, we don't exchange that."

"That's very good, those things are very personal, they only belong to you, you don't give them away and you don't wear somebody else's. The same goes for your undershirt or socks."

"Well, socks keep mixing up because they're small and restless."

They both look at Evi's feet. He's wearing one starry green sock and another with red stripes.

"On second thoughts, Purcelus, I guess I'll manage even if you don't lend me your clothes. And I'll leave this starry sock with you, to keep you company today."

"Thanks. Can't you leave behind something to eat too? Some pea sauce maybe?"

"Sorry, I've got to go, you'll surely find something good in the fridge after my parents go to work."

Evi had a great time on the trip and Purcelus chomped on olives and pressed-cow cheese right in the fridge, where he also fell asleep. Mummy found him there later, he was very cold but snoring happily.

Hey, Kid, Would You Like Us to Be Friends?

One morning Mummy, Evi and the little pig went out to solve some problems. Mummy wanted to go to the post office and send a package to Evi's Granny, who lived far away, in another city. Evi wanted to buy a pretzel from the vendor on the corner and Purcelus wanted to hang from Evi's hand, talking all the time about everything and begging for a piece of pretzel made with sesame.

It didn't take them long to get to the post office. While Mummy was filling out a form for the woman in uniform, Evi sat on a bench next to the window, chewing the hot pretzel, with the little pig lying on his lap and catching with his tongue the sesame seeds which were falling from the pretzel right on his head.

Suddenly a man came up to them. He leant over them and started to whisper to Evi:

"What a cute kid we've got here. How about sharing your pretzel with me?"

Purcelus frowned at him. How rude of him to ask for food from a stranger! It's bad manners!

Evi ignored the man. He kept looking out of the window biting greedily into the pretzel.

Then the man came closer to him and said:

"What if I give you a rock candy? Would you share your pretzel with me then? And make friends with me?"

Purcelus whispered into Evi's ear:

"This man is weird. I suggest you call your Mummy."

Evi winked at him, then shouted at the man so that everybody could hear him, Mummy in particular:

"I hope you don't mind, but Mummy told me not to speak to strangers. You can tell her what you wanted to tell me. Good-bye!"

"Well done, Evi," said Purcelus and shook his hand with his curled tail. "Just the right thing to say. Grown-ups must not talk to children when the latter don't want to and if their Mummies are not with them ... Now, can I have a little bit of that pretzel? Oink?"

Can I Give You a Hug?

Purcelus was being pressed between a big notebook and a bottle of perfume in Mummy's handbag. It was warm in there, the bag was swaying, so he was dozing when all of a sudden he heard children's voices. Evi ran to Mummy, while his mates were shouting *So long, Evi, have a nice weekend, see you Monday.*

Mummy hugged Evi, squeezing Purcelus between them.

"Oink!" he shouted almost choking.

"Oh, sorry, little pig, we didn't want to turn you into a pancake", said Mummy.

"No problem, I like hugs," said the little pig, feeling his belly and tail to make sure they were in one piece and round.

"I for one don't like them too much," said Evi. "Is it bad not to like them?"

"No, my dear. You can hug only those people you want, and only when you feel like it," answered Mummy stroking his head.

"My friends keep hugging each other all the time but I don't want to and don't like to. I don't like to kiss or be kissed either. But when it comes to you, Mummy, I do like to kiss you," said Evi and stuck to her.

"Oink! What about me?" asked the oinking voice from the handbag.

"I didn't like to be touched by others either when I was little," said Mummy, "and Daddy still doesn't like it. You shouldn't worry about it, my little one. It's your body, you decide what to do with it. When you don't want to be touched just say: *I'm sorry, I don't like to be hugged.*"

"Is that all?" asked Evi finding it hard to believe.

"Oink," agreed the little pig.

"I'm glad to hear that, Mummy, I feel more relieved now. It's my body, I say NO whenever I want. I like this rule."

"You should. And one more thing. When somebody else says NO to you, meaning they don't want to be touched or kissed, you must not insist, you must respect their wish."

"Of course, I wouldn't like to be kissed against my will."

"You're a great kid, that's what you are," said Mummy.

"Oink!" came from the handbag. "My body is saying a pizza would make it happy!"

Evi and Mummy burst out laughing. They got into the car, put Purcelus on the backseat, with the seatbelt on, and drove off to town. The pink little pig was smelling all over of Mummy's sweet perfume.

A Message for the Parents

The Naked Truth is a book every family needs to read.

In the amazing and at the same time complex process of bringing children up, parents discover very soon that it is impossible to spend all the time with their little ones. When they are very young, most children are left without their mother and father around for a significant number of hours every working day.

Since children's varied experiences, beyond the door of the house, are not under our control, and children cannot be held captive in a safe and harmonious environment, the only responsible choice is to "equip" them with the attitudes, skills and behavior able to help them stay healthy and safe in most of the situations they may find themselves in at one time or another – especially when their mother and father are not at hand.

With humor and gentleness, Evi and the smart greedy Purcelus invite us to experience with them various familiar and probable events, potentially risky, through which we get information and the necessary steps in dealing with certain situations that we can hardly think of without being worried – inappropriate touches, the protection of their own body, being approached by strangers, getting lost in large public spaces, taking care of their personal objects, the limits of physical manifestations of affection within the family and outside it, etc.

The huge merit of Evi and Purcelus' adventures is that they succeed in showing us, in a way which is far from being panicky, the dangers lurking in the grown-up world where our children grow, offering for each situation, on a playful tone, full of humor and naturalness, the correct information that all parents and children should have. *The Naked Truth* provides simple, efficient solutions that every child can understand, and makes parents more confident that nothing bad will happen to their children when, especially when they are not around.

DIANA STĂNCULESCU,
psychotherapist

Contents

Evi and the Smartest Little Pig 6
Come with Me to the Bathroom! 11
The Secret. 14
On the Beach 17
Later, Curiously 20
In the Park, a Strange Proposal 22
Mummy, Where Are You? 25
An Anniversary Kiss 29
A Bath after the Rain 32
An Exchange of Clothes 36
Hey, Kid, Would You Like Us to Be Friends? 39
Can I Give You a Hug? 41
A Message for the Parents 44

Printed in Great Britain
by Amazon